The 6 Most Important DECISIONS You'll Ever Make

Personal Workbook

SEAN COVEY

A FIRESIDE BOOK
Published by Simon & Schuster
NEW YORK   LONDON   TORONTO   SYDNEY

Fireside
A Division of Simon & Schuster, Inc.
1230 Avenue of the Americas
New York, NY 10020

First Fireside trade paperback edition January 2009

FIRESIDE and colophon are registered trademarks of Simon & Schuster, Inc.

For information about special discounts for bulk purchases, please contact Simon & Schuster Special Sales at 1-800-456-6798 or business@simonandschuster.com.

Manufactured in the United States of America

10 9 8 7 6 5 4 3 2 1

ISBN-13: 978-0-7432-6505-8
ISBN-10:   0-7432-6505-X

This is your book.
Find your favorite picture of yourself and glue it here.

CONTENTS

The Choice Is Yours

Hi, I'm Sean. I guess I could assume since you have this workbook, you have read (or have) my book *The 6 Most Important Decisions You'll Ever Make*. If you've read it, that's great. If you haven't, you can still get great things from this companion workbook. I'm glad you've decided to take the plunge and check this out. I know you'll have fun!

If you haven't heard yet, this book is about one big idea: CHOICE. It's all about the choices you make around six huge decisions you're gonna face during your teen years. These decisions can make or break your future. Pretty heavy stuff. But it's true.

It would be best if you made all the right decisions over the next few years, but if you don't (nobody's perfect, after all!), there is still hope. You can course-correct and get back on track right away. The idea behind this book is to provide you with the tools and information you need to make good choices along the way.

This workbook is designed for you. You can use it any way you want. If you love to write, then just fill in those kinds of activities. If you love to do other things, then do those activities. You don't have to do them all. You can share this book with your friends and family, or you can keep it very private. It's all up to you. Whatever you decide, don't be afraid to mark this workbook up. Write in it. Draw in it. Glue things in it. Mark your favorite pages with sticky notes. This is *your* book.

WHAT ARE THE 6 MOST IMPORTANT DECISIONS YOU'LL EVER MAKE?

After doing a ton of surveys and asking teens all over the world about their biggest challenges, a pattern soon began to emerge. Here are the six challenges that teens mentioned the most. What you do about each of these challenges, incidentally, are the six most important decisions you'll ever make as a teen.

School—I'm Totally Stressed Out! What are you going to do about your education?

 Friends—So Fun . . . So Fickle. What type of friends will you choose and what kind of friend will you be?

 Parents—How Embarrassing! Are you going to get along with your parents?

 Dating & Sex—Do We Have to Talk About This? Who will you date and what will you do about sex?

 Addictions—It's Not Hard to Quit . . . I've Done It a Dozen Times. What will you do about smoking, drinking, drugs, and other addictive stuff?

 Self-Worth—If Only I Were Better Looking. Will you choose to like yourself?

Maybe these are your top six challenges already. Maybe you have others that would be at the top of your list right now. Take a few minutes and think about your top challenges in life. What are they? List a few of them below.

Even if you have other challenges right now, the six we concentrate on in this book are ones that you are probably familiar with. Read the story at the bottom of page 4 in the book and think about how these decisions are like that train switch point. Are you ready to learn how to keep your train going in the right direction? This workbook is going to help you stay on track, so let's get going.

The 7 HABITS

CRASH COURSE

They Make You or Break You

A few years ago, I wrote a book called *The 7 Habits of Highly Effective Teens*. Maybe you've already read it, but if you haven't, here's a quick review. For more detail, read pages 15–32 in the *6 Decisions* book.

Let's talk about paradigms and principles first. A *paradigm* is your perception, point of view, or the way you see the world. We all have them, right or wrong. Have you ever picked up someone else's glasses and put them on? Whoa. Wrong prescription! Those lenses affect how you see the world around you, don't they?

Remember how your ancestors used to think the world was flat? That was a paradigm. It affected how they saw the world (literally!) and how they behaved. Some people thought Columbus was nuts because he wanted to sail to the edge. They believed he would fall off the edge of the world. But he didn't. That was the paradigm shift.

Paradigms are like that. How you see the world affects what you believe, how you think, and how you act. You have paradigms about yourself, other people, and about life in general. If you think you can't do well in school, then you probably won't. If you think you will never get along with your parents, you probably won't. If you think the whole world is against you, you are going to have a hard road ahead. Changing those paradigms takes effort, but it can make all the difference in the world.

Activity: In the space below, write about a time when you had a big paradigm shift. How did it feel? How did it change things for you?

My Big Paradigm Shift

Example: When you were a little kid, you thought your parents were perfect.

when I was a little

What Changed?

If you want to read more, go to page 16 in the *6 Decisions* book.

Activity: Choose a friend or family member and explain the idea about paradigms. Then ask them about a time when they had a paradigm shift and what it was like. You can record below what you found out or draw a picture of the event or just listen as they tell you their story.

Their Story

_____

_____

_____

_____

_____

_____

_____

_____

_____

_____

_____

_____

_____

_____

_____

A *principle* is a natural law. You know—like gravity. Whether you are standing on top of the world or on the bottom, that apple is going to fall. We also have principles that govern our human interactions—things like honesty, trust, patience, service, love, compassion, charity, freedom, wisdom, justice, humor, fairness, and courage.

It takes courage to live by principles. Sure, it's often easier to be dishonest, for example. But in the long run, it will catch up to you. Being honest feels better anyway and will prove your intelligence. Promise.

Principles never fail us. Putting principles first is the key to doing well in all other areas of life.

Activity: In the space below, write down five or six principles. Then number them in the order of their priority in your life.

1. _____

_____

2. _____

_____

3. _____

_____

4. _____

_____

5. _____

_____

6. _____

_____

Activity: Now write down the opposite of those five or six principles you just wrote. Choose one and record what your life would be like if you lived the opposite principle.

Principle:

Living by the principle of _____ would be . . .

_____

_____

_____

_____

_____

_____

_____

_____

_____

_____

_____

_____

If you want to read more about principles, go to page 17 in the *6 Decisions* book.

Activity: In the center of the model below, fill in the principles your life is centered on right now. In the spaces around the center, fill in other important areas of your life.

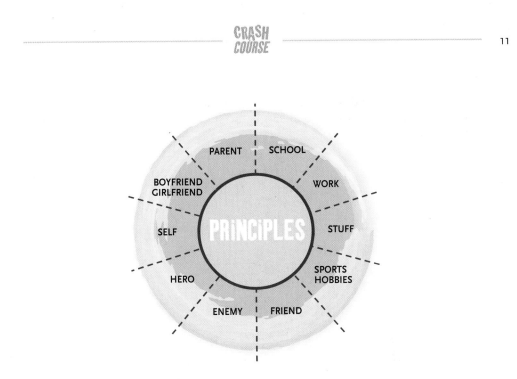

When you put principles at the center of your life, great things start to happen. When you put principles at the center, all the other important things in your life start to fall in place around that.

Each of the 7 Habits is based on timeless principles that never go out of style. Let's quickly check out each one of the habits.

THE 7 HABITS OF HIGHLY EFFECTIVE TEENS

The 7 Habits of Highly Effective Teens are the seven characteristics that happy and successful teens the world over have in common. Here's a list of the habits and quick explanations.

HABIT 1 BE PROACTIVE
Take responsibility for your life.

HABIT 2 BEGIN WITH THE END IN MIND
Define your mission and goals in life.

HABIT 3 PUT FIRST THINGS FIRST
Prioritize, and do the most important things first.

HABIT 4 THINK WIN-WIN
Have an everyone-can-win attitude.

HABIT 5 SEEK FIRST TO UNDERSTAND, THEN TO BE UNDERSTOOD
Listen to people sincerely.

HABIT 6 SYNERGIZE
Work together to achieve more.

HABIT 7 SHARPEN THE SAW
Renew yourself regularly.

So, what would the opposite look like? Read on.

THE 7 HABITS OF HIGHLY *DEFECTIVE* TEENS

HABIT 1   REACT
Don't take responsibility for your life.

HABIT 2   BEGIN WITH NO END IN MIND
Go through life with no mission or goals.

HABIT 3   PUT FIRST THINGS LAST
Stay unorganized and do the unimportant things first.

HABIT 4   THINK WIN-LOSE
Have a win-lose attitude.

HABIT 5   SEEK FIRST TO TALK,
THEN PRETEND TO LISTEN
Don't listen to others sincerely.

HABIT 6   DON'T COOPERATE
Do everything yourself.

HABIT 7   WEAR YOURSELF OUT
Don't renew yourself regularly.

So, which set of habits sounds better to you? On the next few pages, you'll find activities for each habit.

HABIT 1 BE PROACTIVE

Being proactive means thinking before acting and making decisions based on values and principles. Proactive people base their choices on things they can control, not on things they can't.

I don't know about your house, but at mine, whoever has the TV remote is "in control." You could think of your life that way too. You have a remote control. Proactive people carry that remote and use it. If you give away your remote, you allow other people and things to control you.

Activity: Choose one way you are going to "take back your remote" this week. Write it down in the space below. At the end of the week, come back to this spot in the book and record how it went. How did you feel? Consider doing this once a month, or once a week to make even more progress.

How I Will "Take Back the Remote"

Example: I will talk to my brother about borrowing my stuff without asking, rather than freak out at him when he does it.

How Did It Feel to Be Proactive?

What Do I Need to Do So That I Remember to React This Way All the Time?

If you want to read more about Habit 1, go to page 21 in the *6 Decisions* book.

HABIT **2** BEGIN WITH THE END IN MIND

Practicing Habit 2 helps you figure out where you want to go in your life. It's kind of like being the "driver" of your life. You decide your destination and then make sure you have the road map that will get you there. And if you don't decide where you're going, then someone else will!

Activity: Make a road map to your future. You can be as creative as you'd like. One simple way to do this is to draw a timeline and list important events in the past and what you hope to achieve in the future. You could even start it from the day you were born. Where have you been and where are you going? What is your final destination? If that feels too big, draw a map of the current school year. Where did you start? What classes have you taken? What extra-curricular things have you done? And where do you hope to be at the end of the year? Have fun!

Extra Credit! Go to the *6 Decisions* Web site (www.6decisions.com) and write your own mission statement.

If you want to read more about Habit 2, go to page 22 in the *6 Decisions* book.

HABIT 3 PUT FIRST THINGS FIRST

The Time Quadrants model is a great way to visualize how you spend your time. There are two main categories of how we spend time—on important and urgent things or on not important and not urgent things.

The first things are those that mean the most to you—the people and activities that contribute to your mission and your goals. Learning to manage your time and do the most important things first is an essential part of living a successful life.

Urgent things are in your face. They are the activities that demand your attention right now.

Activity: Fill out the Time Quadrants below with the way you spent your time last weekend from Friday night through Sunday night.

THE TIME QUADRANTS

Where Do You Need to Do Some Changing?

If you want to read more about Habit 3, go to page 23 in *6 Decisions* book.

HABIT 4 THINK WIN-WIN

The spirit of win-win is when two people work together to achieve a positive outcome for everyone. When it comes to life, winning isn't everything. But it's a lot! Think about your most important relationships. Are those relationships with people who understand you and help you accomplish your goals?

Activity: Think about a relationship that is really important to you. What makes it a win for you? Find out what makes it a win for the other person.

Relationship

_____

_____

_____

_____

_____

_____

_____

_____

A Win for Me

_____

_____

A Win for the Other Person

If you want to learn more about Habit 4, go to page 25 in the *6 Decisions* book.

HABIT 5 SEEK FIRST TO UNDERSTAND, THEN TO BE UNDERSTOOD

Habit 5 is basically about listening first and talking second. Native Americans use a "talking stick" when they communicate. The person who holds the stick is the only person allowed to speak. When that person feels truly understood, they pass the stick to the next person and it's their turn to talk. Pretty cool concept, isn't it?

Activity: Create your own talking stick, or find an object that will be your family's talking stick. Explain the idea to your parents and ask them to support you in using it when you are all trying to communicate with each other. Try it out at the dinner table. Record how it works out in the space below.

Draw a Picture of the Talking Stick You Created or Found.

If you want to learn more about Habit 5, go to page 26 in the *6 Decisions* book.

HABIT 6 SYNERGIZE

Have you ever worked on a great project with a group of people? Did it just "click" and turn out to be an awesome experience? What about playing on a great sports team? If you have, you have most likely experienced synergy. Synergy is when two or more people or things come together to create something way better than any of them could have created on their own.

The coolest part about synergy is that it's the *differences* that let us work well together, not our similarities. When we work together and listen and respect each others' differences, we become stronger. Celebrating differences is what Habit 6 is about.

Activity: Choose three friends or family members and list how similar they are to you and how different they are from you.

NAME	SIMILARITIES	DIFFERENCES
1.		
2.		
3.		

What Differences Do You Like the Best and Why?

If you want to learn more about Habit 6, go to page 28 in the *6 Decisions* book.

HABIT 7 SHARPEN THE SAW

Habit 7 is the habit of recharging your batteries. Simply put, that means taking care of yourself in the four key dimensions of your life.

Activity: In the model below, fill in the things you do now to renew yourself in each dimension. What new things would you like to try?

Things I Do Now

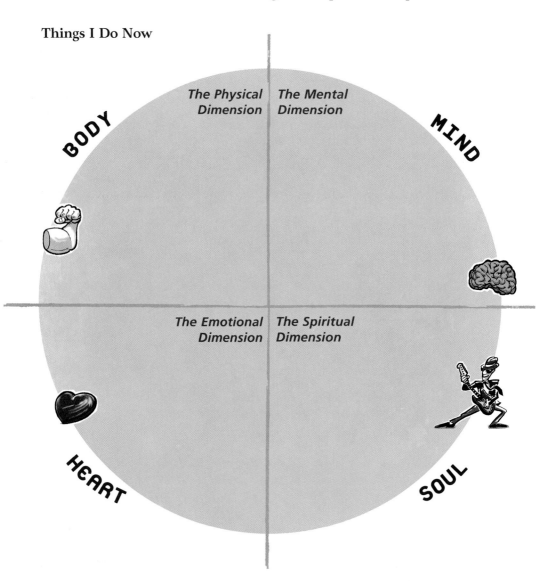

New Things I'd Like to Try

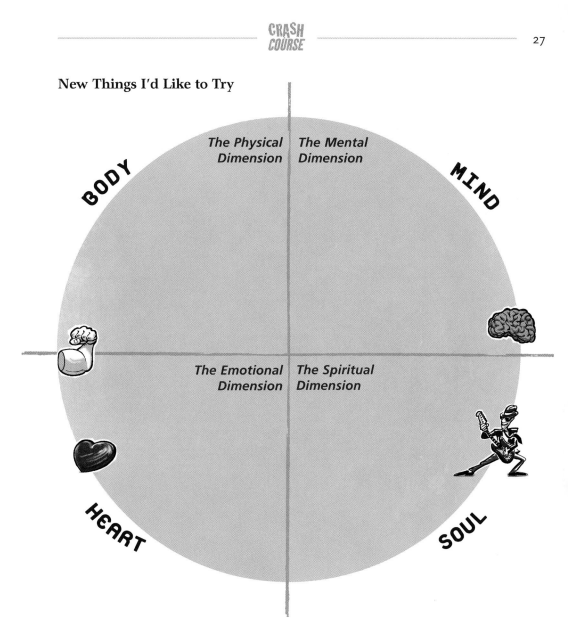

The Physical Dimension

The Mental Dimension

The Emotional Dimension

The Spiritual Dimension

BODY

MIND

HEART

SOUL

If you want to learn more about Habit 7, go to page 29 in the *6 Decisions* book.

MOVING ON

So when are we getting to those 6 Decisions? Right now. Now that you have a good idea of what the 7 Habits are (they'll crop up throughout this workbook), it's time to move on to the next step. Here's how the rest of this workbook is going to be set up.

The first page of every section is going to tell you exactly what you are going to get out of that section. We'll call that "What's in It for Me?"

You're going to see great quotes spread throughout each section. Highlight the ones you really like a lot.

We've also put in the 10-question checkups from the book. If you've already taken them, do them again here and then go back and compare your answers and remind yourself of things you need to work on.

Next are lots of activities and things to do that relate to each decision. Some things might be just for you to think about, some might be things you can go and do.

Toward the end of each section are "Top 10" lists and "Favorite" lists. Fill in the Top 10 items and list your favorite movies, music, TV shows, books, and other things that relate to each decision. Write down uplifting ideas, quotes, stories, or names of people you admire that may help you when times get rough. This is also a great place to write down reminders of things you might want to post on the *6 Decisions* Web site (www.6decisions.com).

At the end of each section, you'll find a checklist. Use it to check off your progress. Did you do the activity? Are you planning on it? When?

DECISION

1

SCHOOL

What's in it
for Me?

1. Sound reasons for sticking it out in school.

2. Ways to stay motivated while coping with the everyday ups and downs of school life.

3. Ways to prepare, get into, and pay for the college of your choice.

4. Help in starting to figure out what you want to be when you grow up.

i made decisions that i regret,
and i took them as learning experiences . . .
i'm human, not perfect, like anybody else.

—Queen Latifah

BRIGHT IDEA!

Since this workbook is focused on *doing*, you aren't going to be given big reading assignments (maybe a few little ones, though) from the book, but don't be afraid to go back and review if you need or want to. It's great reinforcement!

SCHOOL CHECKUP*

When you have choices, you can look at them like forks in the road. A choice is a decision point. In this case, you can take the high road and stay in school, get an education, and lock in your good chances of a fulfilling professional life, or . . . you can take the low road and drop out or not work hard in school.

Which road do you want to take?

---

* To take this checkup or lots of other cool quizzes online, go to www.6decisions.com.

CIRCLE YOUR CHOICE	NO WAY!				HECK YES!
1. I am planning on finishing high school.	1	2	3	4	5
2. I am planning on getting more education after high school.	1	2	3	4	5
3. I believe that a good education is essential to my future.	1	2	3	4	5
4. I am working hard at school.	1	2	3	4	5
5. I am getting good grades.	1	2	3	4	5
6. I am involved in extracurricular activities at school.	1	2	3	4	5
7. I am keeping up with my homework.	1	2	3	4	5
8. I am keeping my stress levels in check.	1	2	3	4	5
9. I am able to balance school with everything else I'm doing.	1	2	3	4	5
10. I spend time thinking about and exploring what I want to be when I grow up.	1	2	3	4	5
TOTAL					

Each of the above questions is worth 5 points, for a total of 50 points. Add up your score and see how you're doing. Remember, this is not a test. It won't be graded. It's simply a self-evaluation to help you assess the choices you're currently making. So don't get all hung up about your score.

You're on the high road. Keep it up!

You're straddling the high and low roads. Move to higher ground!

You're on the low road. Pay special attention to this chapter.

Sticking it Out ──────────
(And I don't mean your tongue!)

Education is not a form of entertainment, but a means of empowering people to take control of their lives.

—Unknown

Remember the example of the marshmallow from the book? Some little kids were given the choice to eat one marshmallow right now or wait for a little while and have two. Some took control of their desire for that soft, sweet marshmallow and waited, while others just couldn't do it. Some stuck it out and some didn't.

That's how it is with school. If you take control of your desire to be doing something more fun for the moment, the payoff in the end is empowerment over how your life turns out. You'll have the skills to choose what you want to do with your life and to get a higher-paying job, which will help you better provide for yourself and your future family. Instead of being stuck doing something you have no passion or desire to do, you have choices.

If you want to learn more, go to pages 37–42 in the *6 Decisions* book.

Activity: If you haven't already decided (and that's probably lots of you), think of a career you might like to pursue. Now go online and find out how much schooling it takes for that job. Then find out how much money you can expect to make when you get out of college.

Hint: Try searching (for example) "lawyer education requirements." Substitute the career you have chosen (teacher, engineer, police officer, Web designer, etc.). You'll find some interesting Web sites with great information.

Career

_____

_____

_____

_____

How Much Schooling Does That Career Require?

Starting Salary

Activity: Make a poster that shows what you can achieve if you stay in school. Brainstorm your ideas and then complete your project on a separate piece of poster board or paper.

Struggling for ideas? Think of things like the kind of job you want to have, where you want to live, or the kind of house you want to live in. If you want, you can make a list below to help you get started.

What I Can Achieve If I Stay in School

_____

_____

_____

_____

_____

_____

_____

_____

_____

_____

_____

Activity: Ask your parents or grandparents about their education. Did they get a high school and college education? Why or why not?

NAME	HIGH SCHOOL?	COLLEGE?	WHY/WHY NOT?

If your family members have a history of not staying in school, how can you break the cycle? List five things you will do starting right now that will help you stick it out.

Five Things That Will Help Me Stick It Out in School

1. Example: I'll go to class.

2.

3.

4.

5.

You can't go through life quitting everything.
if you're going to achieve anything,
you've got to stick with something.

—From the television show *Family Matters*

Surviving and Thriving

(The personal spa treatment)

The troubles of adolescence eventually all go away— it's just like a really long, bad cold.

—Dawn Ruelas

Well maybe, but once you get over the adolescent "cold," the adult "cold" sets in. That's just the way life is sometimes. And stress is a part of life.

This part is mostly about Sharpen the Saw from Habit 7. School is stressful for everyone at one time or another. For some people, it's stressful all the time. But learning how to deal with the stress of school will help you deal with stress everywhere else in your life, which is an important lesson!

Activity: Make a list of healthy ways you can beat school stress.

Healthy Ways to Beat Stress

Examples: Take a walk.

Go to an art museum.

Call Grandma.

If you want to learn more, go to pages 43–65 in the *6 Decisions* book.

Activity: When you are feeling overwhelmed with school, sit down and "free write" for 5–10 minutes. (Don't worry about spelling, grammar, or punctuation—nobody's going to correct this.) Express your feelings and the specific things that are getting you down.

Things That Stress Me About School Right Now

From your comments above, write down the stressful things you feel like you do have control over and the things you don't have control over.

CONTROL   NO CONTROL

Activity: Make a list of at least seven of your favorite (legal, healthy, appropriate) stress relievers. Schedule some specific times to do a few of them over the next week or so.

My Favorite Stress Relievers

Examples: Running

Listening to my favorite CD

Activity: Make yourself a reward jar. It can be any kind of container you want. Think of small rewards you can give yourself for getting all of your homework done, getting enough sleep, staying awake in class, *going* to class.

Write your rewards on little slips of paper and put them in the container. When you feel like you've done a great job in any of your stress areas in school (even a small improvement is worth a reward!), choose a reward and have at it. You deserve it.

When you come to the end of your rope, tie a knot and hang on.

—Franklin D. Roosevelt

Activity: Not enough time to do everything you want and need to do? Did you go through the "Time Finder" activities in the book? Well, here's your second chance. Go to pages 48–51 in the *6 Decisions* book and look for the Time Finder icons. See what you come up with. Record your findings below.

_____

_____

_____

_____

_____

Take some time now to think through what you learned about yourself when you finished the activity. What are you doing well? Where do you need to improve in order to be less stressed out?

What I Do Well

_____

_____

_____

_____

Where I Need to Improve

_____

_____

_____

_____

What motivates you? Have you ever really thought about it?

Activity: Think about the things that motivate you to keep going or to do a great job in school. Make a list and then post it on your mirror or in your planner. Be sure to put it someplace you will see it often. Use the space below to brainstorm ideas.

Things That Motivate Me to Stay in School

Example: Feelings of accomplishment

Activity: In order to stay motivated to do your best in school, it's nice to have an idea of what you are good at. Sometimes those are the things that will motivate you to do well in other areas too. Check out some Web assessments that help you determine your strengths. Here's a suggested site: http://literacy works.org/mi/home.html. It's quick, easy, and it tells you a lot about yourself. Try several.

When you're done, record some of the things you learned about yourself below.

What I Learned About Myself

Activity: Interview a few people with different careers you are interested in. Use the questions below as a starter and then make up more of your own that will give you the information you are looking for.

Why did you choose your career?

_____

_____

_____

_____

_____

How much schooling does it take to be qualified for this job?

_____

_____

_____

_____

_____

What's a typical day like at work?

_____

_____

_____

_____

_____

What's the best part about your job?

_____

_____

_____

_____

_____

What's the worst part about your job?

_____

_____

_____

_____

_____

Additional questions:

_____

_____

_____

_____

_____

To the uneducated, an A is just three sticks.

—A. A. Milne

Finding Your Voice

(Trust me, you don't have to be musical to do this.)

What does it mean to "find your voice"? No, it's not about talking or singing. It's more about the things you love to do—what you were born to do. There are four components to this: talent, passion, need, and conscience. What are you good at? What do you love doing? What does the world need that you could get paid to do? What do you feel you *should* do? Check out how this works when you put all four things together.

Imagine four circles:

What am I really good at?
This is **t a l e n t** .

What do I love doing?
This is **p a s s i o n** .

What does the world need that I can get paid to do?
This is **n e e d** .

What do I feel I should do?
This is **c o n s c i e n c e** .

Activity: Ask your parents or grandparents if they remember things you said when you were a little kid about what you wanted to be when you grew up. Maybe it was something like, "Grandma, I want to do *that* when I get big!" They may have insights on things you have long forgotten that will tap in to finding your voice.

Activity: Make a list of some things you've always wanted to learn.

Things I Want to Learn

   Example: How to throw pottery

Now choose three things from your list and make a plan for when and how you will learn those things.

Top Three Things and My Plan for How to Achieve Them

_____

_____

_____

_____

_____

_____

_____

Extra Credit! Go to the _6 Decisions_ Web site (www.6decisions.com) and share your favorite two activities from this workbook so far.

Activity: Along the same lines, have you ever asked yourself this question: "What would I do if I knew I could not fail?" What if time, experience, and maturity were totally not an issue? Take some time to think about it and write down what you would do.

If I Knew I Could Not Fail, I Would . . .

_____

_____

_____

_____

_____

_____

_____

Activity: Choose someone you trust and share what you wrote. Ask them the same question and see what they say.

BRIGHT IDEA!

See if your local library has a copy of *What Would You Do If You Had No Fear?* by Diane Conway. It's a great book about people who were asked that question and how they responded. Their stories might give you courage to do things you never thought you could!

Off to College

(Are you packed yet?)

The quality of a university is measured more by the kind of student it turns out than the kind it takes in.

—Robert J. Kibbee

Activity: Are you interested in going to college or a vocational training school? If so, search for schools that meet your needs and have degrees or training in the field you are interested in—there may be several to choose from. Try a search on the Web or in your counseling office. See what you come up with. Write down the ones that interest you and the ones that you are eligible for.

Field I Am Interested In

School

School

_____

_____

_____

School

_____

_____

_____

MAKE AN APPOINTMENT

Activity: Make an appointment with your school counselor and get as much information as you can about scholarships and how to get them. Even if you don't get every scholarship you apply for, this is great practice for future job interviews. Filling out a scholarship application helps you to focus on your strengths and defines your ambitions.

Date I Will Meet with My School Counselor

_____

Scholarships I Could Apply For

_____

_____

_____

_____

_____

What I Need to Do to Apply

_____

_____

_____

Activity: Make a calendar (or mark in your planner, cell phone, or computer) with milestone dates for applying for scholarships, qualifying tests, interviews, school applications, and onsite visits to check out schools you may want to attend.

S	M	T	W	TH	F	S

A good mind is a terrible thing to waste, and you have a good mind! As hard as it may be at times, staying in school and feeding your mind is what taking the high road means when it comes to the first most important decision you'll ever make. If you've been struggling, it's never too late to get back on track and get that diploma. Hang in there and put on your hiking boots. Then choose the high road.

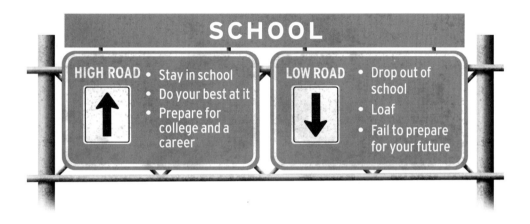

Top 10 Lists

Top 10 School Challenges

Top 10 Things I Like About School

Top 10 Things to Do Before College

My Top 10 . . .

Favorite Lists

Favorite Movies About School

Favorite Songs About School

Favorite Movie, TV Show, or Book About School

HOW AM I DOING?

CHECK YOUR CHOICE	TO DO	DOING	DONE
School Checkup	☐	☐	☐
Career Activity	☐	☐	☐
What I Can Achieve If I Stay in School	☐	☐	☐
Family School History	☐	☐	☐
Five Things That Will Help Me Stick It Out in School	☐	☐	☐
Healthy Ways to Beat School Stress	☐	☐	☐
Things That Stress Me About School Right Now	☐	☐	☐
Control/No Control	☐	☐	☐
My Favorite Stress Relievers	☐	☐	☐
Reward Jar	☐	☐	☐
Time Finder	☐	☐	☐
What I Do Well	☐	☐	☐
Things That Motivate Me to Stay in School	☐	☐	☐
What I Learned About Myself	☐	☐	☐
Career Interviews	☐	☐	☐
Finding My Voice	☐	☐	☐
Things I Want to Learn	☐	☐	☐
Achievement Plan	☐	☐	☐
If I Knew I Could Not Fail, I Would . . .	☐	☐	☐
Field I Am Interested In	☐	☐	☐
Make an Appointment	☐	☐	☐
Make a Calendar	☐	☐	☐

DECISION 2

FRiENDS

So Fun... So Fickle

What's in it
for Me?

1. Ways to survive the everyday ups and downs of friendships.

2. Ideas on making and being a good friend.

3. Ways to resist peer pressure and build your own positive support system.

Hold a true friend with both your hands.

—Nigerian proverb

BRIGHT IDEA!

If you haven't done it already, give a copy of this book or the *6 Decisions* book to a good friend so you can both do the activities and then talk about what you've learned.

Friends . . .

So Fun . . . So Fickle

There's nothing better than having a best friend, no matter how old you are. We all want them. We all need them. So why is it sometimes so hard to find good friends—the ones who build you up, help you through the tough times, and are fun to be with?

Maybe it's hard to tell who is going to be there through anything and who is just there while things are good. Maybe it's because you don't always know whether someone will be a good friend or a bad friend until you've spent a lot of time with them. Or maybe it's just because there are so many people out there to choose from! Figuring out who will be a good friend is a big decision. And it's not a single decision. It's a series of decisions made over and over again as time goes on.

Try some of the activities and ideas in this section that will help you learn how to make and keep good friends.

FRIENDS CHECKUP

CIRCLE YOUR CHOICE	NO WAY!				HECK YES!
1. I have at least one or more true friends.	1	2	3	4	5
2. I make an effort to get to know new people and make new friends.	1	2	3	4	5
3. The friends I hang out with are a positive influence on me.	1	2	3	4	5
4. I'm inclusive of others and don't belong to an exclusive clique.	1	2	3	4	5
5. I don't judge other people before I get to know them.	1	2	3	4	5
6. I'm loyal to my friends and don't talk behind their backs.	1	2	3	4	5
7. I'm quick to forgive my friends when they make mistakes.	1	2	3	4	5
8. I'm a good listener and don't dominate discussions.	1	2	3	4	5
9. I'm kind to everyone, not just people I like.	1	2	3	4	5
10. I am able to resist peer pressure and be my own person.	1	2	3	4	5
TOTAL					

Add up your score and see how you're doing.

 40-50 You're on the high road. Keep it up!

 30-39 You're straddling the high and low roads. Move to higher ground!

 10-29 You're on the low road. Pay special attention to this chapter.

Surviving the Everyday Ups and Downs of Friendships ———

(Fasten your seat belt and keep your hands and arms inside the ride at all times!)

Feel like you never know what to expect from day to day when it comes to your friends? Is *your* life pretty up and down? Well, guess what? So is theirs. So before you get all upset and crown your friend "Dork for the Day," try this next activity.

Activity: Draw or take pictures of friends you really admire. Make a scrapbook page and write down next to each picture why you admire them.
Or simply list them below.

MY FRIENDS

WHY I ADMIRE THEM

1. _____

1. _____

_____

_____

_____

_____

_____

_____

2. _____

2. _____

_____

_____

_____

_____

3. _____   3. _____

_____   _____

_____   _____

_____   _____

4. _____   4. _____

_____   _____

_____   _____

_____   _____

5. _____   5. _____

_____   _____

_____   _____

_____   _____

**A successful person is one who can
lay a firm foundation with the bricks
that others throw at him or her.**

—David Brinkley

If you want to learn more, go to pages 93–104 in the *6 Decisions* book.

The ups and downs of friendship aren't always centered on your needs. Sometimes your friends need you. It's a two-way street—kind of like being on a teeter-totter. If you both work at it, you can stay balanced.

Activity: Who are some of your friends that could use some help? Take a few minutes and come up with some ways you could help them.

How I Can Help

_____

_____

_____

_____

_____

Now call, text message, or go see your friend to offer your help. Remember, it doesn't have to be a big thing. It could be something as "small" as just lending a listening ear. Make sure whatever you do is a deposit for that person!

Have you ever thought to yourself, "I wish my friends would just like me for who I am"? We all have felt that way at one time or another.

So, what can you do about it? Try the activity below.

Activity: Pretend you're meeting yourself for the first time. What good qualities do you see right away? Put a checkmark next to all of the qualities that your friends appreciate. What are some things your friends expect from you that aren't true to your personality?

MY GOOD QUALITIES   **APPRECIATED?**

_____   _____

_____   _____

_____   _____

_____   _____

Think of a few friends. What would they say your best qualities are?

FRIEND   **WHAT THEY'D SAY (GOOD)**

Activity: Have you ever thought about why you chose your friends, and why they chose you?

In the space below, list some of your friends and then list the reasons you like them. Think of some of the principles they live by. Then ask your friends to list their reasons for being *your* friend.

You were born an original. Don't die a copy.

—John Mason

Popularity is a big issue, in school and out. If you are popular, sometimes you wish you weren't. If you aren't, sometimes it can feel like you should do anything to be one of the popular kids. For some, making friends is a piece of cake. For others it's like pulling teeth. Everyone is trying to find their place and feel accepted. But it's important to choose the right friends and that you choose to be a good friend in the process. So, what makes someone popular anyway? Can you tell just by looking at someone? Try this next activity and see what you find out.

Activity: Go to the mall or some other busy place where kids hang out. Now just sit and watch people, both young and old. Check out facial expressions, body language, the way they walk, gestures, what they wear. Can you tell who's popular and who's not? Why or why not? What does "popular" really mean to you? Does it mean something else to other people? Share some of your feelings and what you learned during your people-watching time.

What Made Me Think Some Were Popular Whereas Others Were Not?

_____

_____

_____

_____

What I Learned by Watching People

_____

_____

_____

_____

Be who you are and say what you feel, because those who mind don't matter and those who matter don't mind.

—Dr. Seuss

Have you ever been the target of a bully, been gossiped about, or treated rudely? You may want to read pages 100–102 in the *6 Decisions* book to remind yourself of some of the things you can do about it.

Have You Ever Been Bullied? How Did It Make You Feel?

_____

_____

_____

_____

_____

_____

_____

Have You Ever Been a Bully? How Did It Make You Feel?
How Do You Think It Made the Other Person Feel?

_____

_____

_____

_____

_____

_____

Activity: Think of some movies, TV shows, or cartoons that have bullies in them.

Draw Your Own Cartoon Bully.

Some people come into our lives
and quickly go.
Some stay for a while and leave
footprints on our hearts.
And we are never, ever the same.

—Anonymous

Life is about change, isn't it? Times change, people change, situations change. So, does that mean if your friend from first grade doesn't want to hang with you anymore that you've done something wrong? Not necessarily. Read on.

Activity: Decide to meet a new person at regular intervals. It can be once a month, once a week, or even once a day—you decide how often and how many. Introduce yourself to someone at school, church, or in your neighborhood—someone who is part of your regular routine but who you have never taken time to get to know. New kid sitting alone at lunch? Be the first one to offer friendship. It'll make your day!

Activity: This week meet five new people. Write down their names and where you met them.

1. _____ _____

2. _____ _____

3. _____ _____

4. _____ _____

5. _____ _____

Making and Being a Friend
(It goes both ways.)

You have been my friend. That in itself is a tremendous thing.
I wove my webs for you because I liked you.
After all, what's a life, anyway? We're born, we live a little while,
we die. A spider's life can't help being something of a mess,
with all this trapping and eating flies.
By helping you, perhaps I was trying to lift up
my life a trifle. Heaven knows
anyone's life can stand a little of that.

—Charlotte, *Charlotte's Web*, E. B. White

Activity: Can you be like Charlotte and start giving to others? Here are some ideas to get you started. Use the space below to think of your own ideas.

- Be the first one to talk to the new kid at school.

- Call a friend who is struggling or feeling down. Get them to go for a bike ride or run with you.

When a friend is in trouble, don't annoy him by asking if there is anything you can do. Think up something appropriate and do it.

—Edgar Watson Howe

If you want to learn more, go to pages 104–113 in the *6 Decisions* book.

You know how easy it is to say, "Let me know if I can do anything to help you." We do it all the time. But guess what? Most people aren't going to let you know. So it's up to you to be proactive and jump in when you see a need. It's kind of like the phrase "Sense a need, fill a need." (Friends aren't the only ones who could use a little help once in a while! Those other people in your house might be in need too.)

Activity: Think about someone in your life who is struggling right now. Think of one concrete thing you can do to lift that person's load. Now go *do it*. Right now!

What I Can Do to Help

Activity: Make a poster of the seven essentials of being a good friend and post it in your room.

1. Be slow to judge.
2. Make the effort.
3. Build the RBA—the Relationship Bank Account is just like a regular bank account. When it comes to relationships, you make deposits or with-drawals into other people's accounts and they make them into yours.
4. Be more open to doing things that others want to do instead of only doing things you want to do.
5. Be inclusive.
6. Treat unkindness with kindness.
7. Lift others.

Peer Pressure

(The good, the bad, and the ugly)

if all my friends were to jump off a bridge,
i wouldn't jump with them.
i'd be at the bottom to catch them.

—Tim McGraw

There are two kinds of peer pressure: positive and negative. Most of the time we hear about the negative kind, but it's not that hard to avoid if you are prepared. Once you prepare yourself, you can start being a force for good and be a promoter of positive peer pressure.

Activity: You can use the idea of the Peer Pressure Shield to help you get there by identifying your support system and then having courage in the moment.

My Support System

_____

_____

_____

_____

_____

_____

_____

_____

What I Will Do in the Moment

_____

_____

_____

_____

_____

_____

_____

_____

If you want to learn more, go to pages 113–122 in the _6 Decisions_ book.

2dh

70

Activity: Think about a time in the past when you gave in to negative peer pressure. How did it make you feel? What are you doing to make sure you never fall into that trap again?

Why Did I Give In to Peer Pressure? What Things Made Me Feel Like I Had to Do Something?

Draw a Picture of How It Made You Feel.

What I Plan to Do in the Future When Faced with Peer Pressure

_____

_____

_____

_____

_____

_____

_____

_____

Activity: Make a list of your top five ways to say no to peer pressure. Keep it with you and read it often or post it in your locker or on the mirror in your bathroom or bedroom.

Top Five Ways to Say No

1. Example: I don't think so!

_____

2. _____

_____

3. _____

_____

4. _____

_____

5. _____

_____

Activity: Get together with two or three friends. Decide together the things you will stand for and specific things you will and will not do. Keep this list in a safe place and refer to it often.

My Friends

What We Stand For

1. Example: Healthy body and mind

2.

3.

4.

What We Will Do

1. Example: Exercise and eat right

2.

3. _____

_____

_____

4. _____

_____

_____

What We Won't Do

1. Example: We will not smoke

_____

2. _____

_____

_____

3. _____

_____

_____

4. _____

_____

_____

Learn to be a leader. Even though you may prefer being a team player, developing leadership skills will help you make good choices in the hard moments. Having those skills can also help you influence others for good.

Activity: List ways you can be a leader at school, home, teams, church. Choose two things from your list that you really want to do, check them off, and follow through on your choice.

Ways I Can Be a Leader

❏ Join a service club at school.

❏ Read to kids at the library.

❏ Be part of the student council.

❏ Add your own:

_____

_____

_____

Bet you never thought there was so much to choosing, making, and being a friend, did you? Making and keeping friends may not sound that hard, but the reason we've talked so much about it is because friends really deserve to be one of the 6 Most Important Decisions You'll Ever Make. Because our friends can have a lot of impact on us, choosing the high road here is really important. Choose friends who impact you for good and help you become the person you really want to be. It will be worth it!

FRIENDS

HIGH ROAD
• Choose friends that build you up
• Be a true friend
• Stand up to peer pressure

LOW ROAD
• Choose friends that bring you down
• Be a fickle friend
• Give in to peer pressure

Top 10 Lists

Top 10 Ways I Can Be a Good Friend

Top 10 Great Things My Friends Do for Me

Top 10 Things to Do with My Friends

My Top 10 . . .

Favorite Lists

Favorite Movies About Friends

Favorite Songs About Friends

Favorite Friend Quotes

HOW AM I DOING?

CHECK YOUR CHOICE	TO DO	DOING	DONE
Friends Checkup	☐	☐	☐
Friends I Admire	☐	☐	☐
How I Can Help	☐	☐	☐
Qualities of a Friend	☐	☐	☐
People-watching	☐	☐	☐
Draw Your Own Cartoon Bully	☐	☐	☐
Meet New People	☐	☐	☐
Giving to Others	☐	☐	☐
Lift That Person's Load	☐	☐	☐
Seven Essentials of Being a Good Friend	☐	☐	☐
Facing Negative Peer Pressure	☐	☐	☐
Peer Pressure Support System	☐	☐	☐
Ways to Say No	☐	☐	☐
What We Stand For	☐	☐	☐
Learn to Be a Leader	☐	☐	☐

DECISION
3

PARENTS

HOW EMBARRASSING!

What's in it
for Me?

1. Great ways to build better relationships with my parents.

2. Ideas for coping with those annoying and upsetting things my parents do.

3. Ways to close that gigantic communication gap between me and my parents.

4. Suggestions for dealing with parents who have lost control of their own lives.

My parents always told me i could be anything i wanted. When you grow up in a household like that, you learn to believe in yourself.

—Rick Schroeder

BRIGHT IDEA!
If your parents gave you my *6 Decisions* book or this workbook but have no idea what it's about, bookmark your favorite spots and ask them to read it. You could even try reading it together.

Parents . . . How Embarrassing!

So, what *are* you going to do about your relationship with your parents? The people in your life who fill the parental role are in it for the long run. Isn't it worth it to make it the best it can be?

Having a good relationship with your parents takes work from both parties. If you are struggling with this, it might take a little bit more work than if everything is going great right now. That's okay. It will be worth it in the end. Keep reading to find some great ideas for things you can personally do to build a better relationship with your parents, as well as things you can help *them* do to get to know you better.

 **PARENTS CHECKUP**

CIRCLE YOUR CHOICE	NO WAY!				HECK YES!
1. I have a good relationship with my parents.	1	2	3	4	5
2. I show my parents respect.	1	2	3	4	5
3. My parents trust me.	1	2	3	4	5
4. I frequently help out my parents without being asked.	1	2	3	4	5
5. I know a lot about my parents, such as their likes, dislikes, dreams, values, and what makes them tick.	1	2	3	4	5
6. My parents know a lot about me, such as my likes, dislikes, dreams, values, and what makes me tick.	1	2	3	4	5
7. My parents and I communicate well with each other.	1	2	3	4	5
8. We are pretty good at solving problems or conflicts.	1	2	3	4	5
9. If and when we do fight or argue, my parents and I make up pretty quickly.	1	2	3	4	5
10. I can honestly say that I love my parents.	1	2	3	4	5
TOTAL					

Add up your score and see how you're doing.

 You're on the high road. Keep it up!

 You're straddling the high and low roads. Move to higher ground!

 You're on the low road. Pay special attention to this chapter.

While we try to teach our children all about life,
our children teach us what life is all about.

—Anonymous

The Relationship Bank Account

(With branches all over the world!)

The Relationship Bank Account is just like a regular bank account. When it comes to relationships, you make deposits or withdrawals into other people's accounts and they make them into yours. You do this with everybody, but right now let's think about your Relationship Bank Account with your parents.

Activity: Begin with the end in mind. Think about your life today, and then try to think about what it will be like 20 years from now. In the space below, describe what your ideal relationship with your parents will look like. Then list three things you can do right now to put yourself on the path to achieving that ideal relationship.

What an Ideal Relationship with My Parents Looks Like

Today

_____

_____

_____

20 Years from Now

_____

_____

_____

Three Things I Can Do Right Now to Create an Ideal Relationship

1.

2.

3.

If you want to learn more, go to pages 130–136 in the *6 Decisions* book.

Do you know what things make a deposit in your Relationship Bank Account with your parents? Do they know what a deposit is for you? They probably are not the same things! It's important to know what kinds of deposits are important and special to the other people around you. There are many ways to find out what a deposit is for your parents (it might not be the same for your dad as it is for your mom!). You can watch and listen, but here's another way to figure it out. Try this activity and see how you do.

Activity: Fill out both columns and then show it to your parents. Were you right about them? Were they surprised about your list?

A DEPOSIT FOR MY PARENTS	A DEPOSIT FOR ME

"So how was your day?"
"Fine."
"What interesting things did you learn in school today?
"Nothing."

How many times have you had that "conversation" with a parent? Probably a million. I guess you could look at it as your parents butting into your life, but the reality is that they are just interested in *you*.

Activity: For one week, make a promise to yourself that you will respond to the questions your parents ask you with complete sentences of four or more words.

Activity: Every day for one week, look around at home and "sense the need." If your parents are having a hard day, ask how you can help, or just step up and do one small thing that you already know would make them happy and be a deposit for them.

In the space below, draw a picture of your parents' reaction or write what you think will happen in your relationship. Come back in a week and see if you were right.

You're So Annoying

(You want to see annoying? I'll show you annoying!)

Activity: Make a list of the top five ways parents can be annoying, then show it to your parents. Thank them for all the ways they do *not* embarrass you. Then ask if you can talk about the ways that they do. (Always start with the positive, it's a great way to make people listen!) Work together to find ways to avoid the situations when they embarrass you and record them below.

Ways My Parents Embarrass Me

_____

_____

_____

_____

_____

Now ask them to commit to avoiding embarrassing moments.

I Will Try My Hardest to Avoid Embarrassing My Child by . . .

_____

_____

_____

_____

_____

Parent's signature   Date

If you want to learn more, go to pages 136–146 in the *6 Decisions* book.

Controlling and overprotective parents? Are you sure they're really *trying* to be that way? Or do they just care about you?

Activity: Next time you're with your mom or dad, or both, ask them their honest reasons for why they set the curfews they do, or why they ask your friends such embarrassing questions, or why they make so many rules. You may be surprised at their answers. Record them below with your thoughts on how you may have had a paradigm shift!

MY PARENTS' RULES	WHY I THINK THEY SET THEM	WHY THEY *REALLY* SET THEM

i don't know any parents that look into the eyes of a newborn baby and say, "How can we mess this kid up."

—Russell Bishop

Have you ever felt like your mom and dad are ruining your life? that they don't care about you because if they did, they would never treat you the way that they do? Picture what it might have been like the day you were born. Can you even imagine your parents thinking about how they would *plan* to mess you up? Of course you can't. But you didn't arrive with an owner's manual in your hand either! If anyone's messed up, they probably feel like it's them most of the time.

Activity: Make up *your* unique owner's manual. What do your parents need to know about you so they can finish raising you? It can be serious or funny, or a little bit of both.

Here's a quick example:

OWNER'S MANUAL
FOR _____
RULE #1 _____
RULE #2 _____
RULE #3 _____
RULE #4 _____

Example: Rule 1. Feed often with yummy food.

Now let's take that owner's manual idea a step further. How about an owner's manual for your parents?

Activity: Present this to your parents and ask them to come up with their own owner's manual.

OWNER'S MANUAL

FOR _____

RULE #1 _____

RULE #2 _____

RULE #3 _____

RULE #4 _____

Example: Rule 1. To frustrate, roll eyes as a response.

Closing the Gap

(Don't worry, it won't take braces.)

You and your parents are not from two different planets. It just feels that way at times. You speak one language, but the words that come out of their mouths in response sound like something from some other planet. And it's the same thing from their perspective too. What to do? Read on.

Activity: Getting to know each other better really does help. Take the following quizzes with your parents and see how you do.

How Well Do You Know YOUR MOM/DAD?

1. What color are your mom's/dad's eyes? _____

2. What is your mom's/dad's favorite thing to do? _____

   _____

3. What would your mom/dad consider to be the nicest thing you could do for her/him? _____

   _____

4. If your mom/dad had all the time and money in the world, what would they spend their time doing? _____

   _____

5. What are your mom's/dad's views on marriage? _____

   _____

6. What is your mom's/dad's greatest unfulfilled dream? _____

   _____

7. What was your mom's/dad's first full-time job? _____

8. Who is your mom's/dad's closest friend? _____

9. How did your parents first meet? _____

   _____

10. What is your mom's/dad's favorite kind of music? _____

11. What is your mom's/dad's favorite TV show? _____

12. Who did your mom/dad vote for in the last election? _____

13. Does your mom/dad gas up the car when the tank is half empty or wait until it is nearly empty? _____

14. Where is your mom's/dad's favorite vacation spot? _____

    _____

15. What would your mom/dad rather do: watch a good TV show, go out to the movies, go to dinner with some friends, or read a book? _____

    _____

How Well Do You Know YOUR TEEN?

1. What is your teen's favorite subject in school? _____

2. What would your teen consider to be the nicest thing you could do for him/her? _____

3. What would your teen like to become when he/she grows up? _____

4. What is your teen's favorite kind of music? _____

5. What is your teen's hot button, the thing that really makes him/her mad?

   _____

6. What is your teen's favorite Internet site? _____

7. What is the one thing your teen wishes he/she could change about himself or herself? _____

8. What would your teen really like to talk about with you, but is afraid to?

   _____

9. What pet would your teen prefer to have: a dog, a cat, a hamster, a horse, a bird, a turtle, a snake, no pet at all, or all of the above? _____

10. Who is your teen's best friend? _____

11. If your teen could travel anywhere in the world, where would he/she go?

    _____

12. What would your teen rather do: go to a movie with friends, read a good book, play games on the computer, or play his/her favorite sport? _____

13. Does your teen have a boyfriend or girlfriend right now? If so, who is it?

    _____

14. What has been one of the high points of your teen's life so far?

    _____

15. What was your teen's favorite vacation ever? _____

    _____

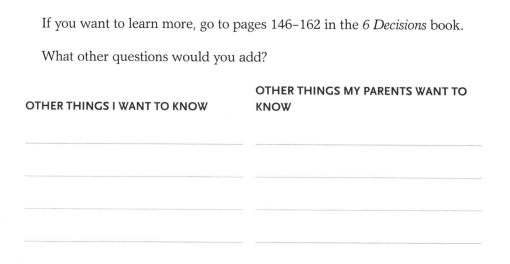

If you want to learn more, go to pages 146–162 in the *6 Decisions* book.

What other questions would you add?

OTHER THINGS I WANT TO KNOW	OTHER THINGS MY PARENTS WANT TO KNOW

When you and your parents disagree on something, use the Getting to Synergy Action Plan.

Activity: Think of a conflict you are having with your parents right now, like curfews or sharing the car. Use the Getting to Synergy Action Plan below to resolve it.

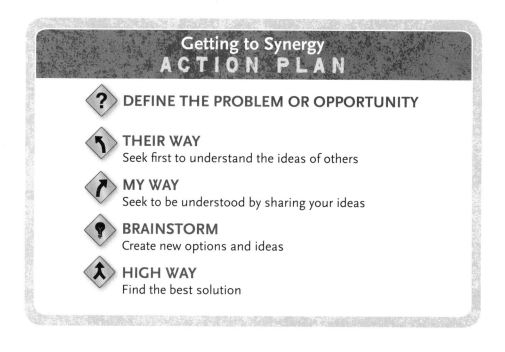

Getting to Synergy
ACTION PLAN

? DEFINE THE PROBLEM OR OPPORTUNITY

THEIR WAY
Seek first to understand the ideas of others

MY WAY
Seek to be understood by sharing your ideas

BRAINSTORM
Create new options and ideas

HIGH WAY
Find the best solution

When You Have to Raise Your Parents —
(Talk about a role reversal!)

Nobody's perfect—least of all your parents. That doesn't make it any easier for you to realize that your parents—the people you thought were perfect just a few years ago—have messed up things in their own lives. But there are ways you can help them and help yourself through this.

Activity: Read the story about Liz Murray on pages 164–165 in the *6 Decisions* book. If Liz can do it, so can you! Take some time really to think about what steps you can take to create a better life for yourself. They don't have to be huge things. Sometimes the little things count the most!

Activity: If your family is short on expressions of love, be a cycle-breaker. Give each member of your family a hug and say, "I love you," each day for a week. You may get funny looks at first, but don't let that stop you. You'll be amazed at the difference!

Things I Can Do to Show Love

_____

_____

_____

_____

_____

_____

_____

_____

_____

If you want to learn more, go to pages 162–167 in the *6 Decisions* book.

Activity: Make a list of three people you really trust, including at least one adult. Then write down a list of things you are really concerned about in your life. Even if you are scared or embarrassed, talk to one of the people on your trusted-people list about your concerns. Brainstorm together the things you can do to keep yourself afloat. Share your thoughts and feelings below.

People I Trust

_____

_____

_____

My Biggest Concerns

_____

_____

_____

Things I Can Do

_____

_____

_____

Extra Credit! Go to the *6 Decisions* Web site (www.6decisions.com) and share some of the things you've learned so far.

Activity: Do a search on the Web for helpful ideas on how to deal with your situation. Share them with one of the other people on your "People I Trust" list.

Other Helpful Ideas

Person I Will Share Them With

Activity: In your journal, planner, cell phone, or computer, record the phone numbers of any help lines you may need. Look up local phone numbers for groups that could help and add them to your list. Don't be afraid to call! That's what they are for—to help *you*.

You and your parents are pretty much stuck with each other, right? So why not make the best of it and decide to take the high road right now? Working together now to build the relationship you want for the future will be totally worth it. I never said it was going to be easy, but it will be worth it. You will be amazed at the difference it makes when you choose the high road and show your love and respect for your parents right now. A good relationship is a process—a path—so choose the higher path and go for it!

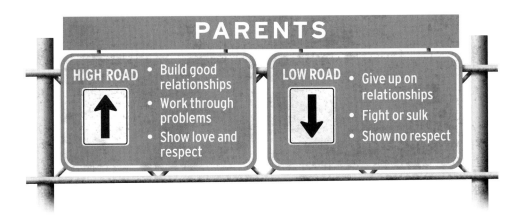

Top 10 Lists

Top 10 Ways My Parents Annoy Me

Top 10 Ways I Annoy My Parents

Top 10 Things My Parents and I Can Do to Be Nicer to Each Other (Here's one to do together!)

My Top 10 . . .

Favorite Lists

Favorite Movies About Families

Favorite Music About Families

Favorite Sayings or Quotes About Parents/Families

Favorite Memories with My Parents

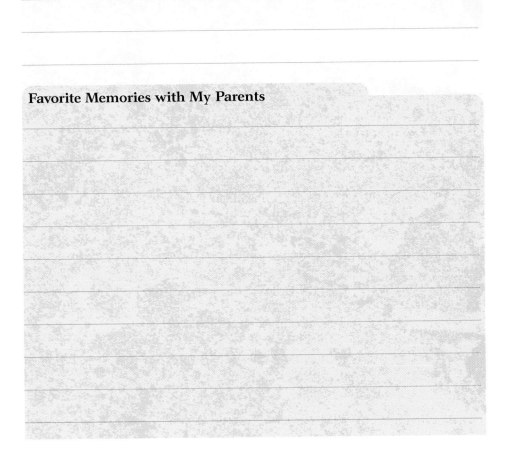

HOW AM I DOINC?

CHECK YOUR CHOICE	TO DO	DOING	DONE
Parents Checkup	☐	☐	☐
Ideal Relationship	☐	☐	☐
Relationship Bank Account	☐	☐	☐
Responding to Parents	☐	☐	☐
Sensing the Need	☐	☐	☐
You're So Annoying	☐	☐	☐
Parents' Rules	☐	☐	☐
Your Owner's Manual	☐	☐	☐
Your Parents' Owner's Manual	☐	☐	☐
Getting to Know You	☐	☐	☐
Getting to Synergy Action Plan	☐	☐	☐
Steps to a Better Life	☐	☐	☐
Things I Can Do to Show Love	☐	☐	☐
People I Trust	☐	☐	☐
Share Ideas	☐	☐	☐
Helpful Numbers	☐	☐	☐

What's in it
for Me?

1. Ways to be successful at dating, being selective about who you date, hanging out and having fun, remaining steady through the natural highs and lows of romance, and keeping your own standards.

2. Information about the Four Great Sex Myths.

3. The meaning of true love.

BRIGHT IDEA!

If you have a friend who's really struggling with this whole dating thing, take a moment with them and share what you've learned. You never know if just one thing you share will help make all the difference in the world.

Dating and Sex—Do We Have to Talk About This?

Dating. Such a simple word, and yet one filled with excitement, fear, and uncertainty. It's different for everyone. Some people sail through the experience seemingly unscathed. For others, it's nothing but one drama after another. Which one do you want it to be? You do have a choice, you know!

As I said in the *6 Decisions* book, what you do in your romantic relationships is probably the most important decision you will make as a teen. Why? Because this choice affects so many other people besides yourself. Dating might seem like a simple decision, but it can have major consequences down the road. Make poor choices here and it affects you, your boyfriend or girlfriend, your parents, your friends, and your siblings.

In real love, you want the other person's good.
In romantic love, you want the other person.

—Margaret Anderson

DATING AND SEX CHECKUP

CIRCLE YOUR CHOICE	NO WAY!				HECK YES!
1. I carefully choose who I go out with and don't date just anybody.	1	2	3	4	5
2. I have decided beforehand what I will and won't do on a date.	1	2	3	4	5
3. My relationships with the opposite sex are based upon genuine friendship, not just the physical side of things.	1	2	3	4	5
4. I feel good about the decisions I'm making when it comes to dating and sex.	1	2	3	4	5
5. My romantic relationships are healthy.	1	2	3	4	5
6. I'm well informed about STDs, pregnancy, and the emotional risks of having sex.	1	2	3	4	5
7. I have not centered my life on a boyfriend or girlfriend.	1	2	3	4	5
8. I have the courage to say *no* to things I don't want to do.	1	2	3	4	5
9. I treat my body with respect.	1	2	3	4	5
10. I'm waiting until I'm in a long-term, committed relationship before having sex.	1	2	3	4	5
TOTAL					

Add up your score and see how you're doing.

 40-50 You're on the high road. Keep it up!

 30-39 You're straddling the high and low roads. Move to higher ground!

 10-29 You're on the low road. Pay special attention to this chapter.

DATING•SEX
4

intelligent Dating ────────────────

(Is there really such a thing?)

Part of intelligent dating is being realistic about romance. Is that really possible when it's so easy to get all sappy about it?

Activity: Pick a romantic scene from one of your favorite movies and watch it by yourself or with a friend. When it's over, talk about or write down why you think it's so romantic. Decide if the scene is realistic or not. Do you think it's possible for the same things to happen in a real-life relationship? Why or why not? What did you learn?

Movie I Watched

_____

Romantic Moments

_____

_____

Realistic? Why or Why Not?

_____

_____

What Did I Learn?

_____

_____

If you want to learn more, go to pages 173–195 in the *6 Decisions* book.

Activity: In the spaces below, respond to the 6 Universal Dating Questions with your personal thoughts on each one.

What Do I Expect?

_____

_____

_____

_____

_____

Who Do I Want to Go Out With? Why?

_____

_____

_____

_____

_____

How Important Is Dating to Me? Why?

_____

_____

_____

_____

_____

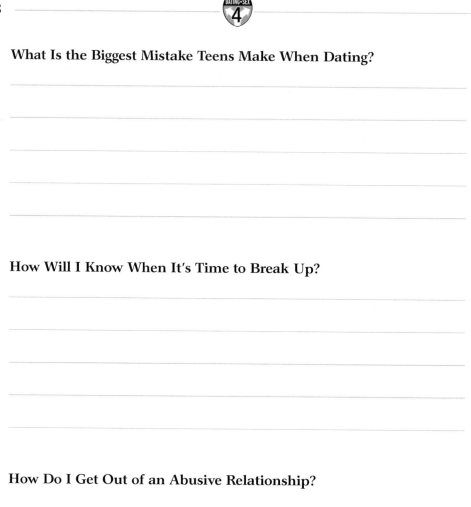

What Is the Biggest Mistake Teens Make When Dating?

How Will I Know When It's Time to Break Up?

How Do I Get Out of an Abusive Relationship?

Activity: If your family owns a video camera or your cell phone has video recording, create a dating-game show and interview four or five people, male and female. Ask them to describe their "perfect date." Make a list of about three questions you want to ask so that you get a clear description of what the person looks like, their personality, etc. Have fun and see what you come up with!

Interview Questions

1. _____

_____

2. _____

_____

3. _____

_____

Activity: Ask several adults, including your parents, what their dating experiences were like. What advice would they give you that might help you right now? What would they change if they could go back? Use the space below to capture what they tell you.

Their Advice

_____

_____

_____

_____

_____

_____

Love is like playing the piano. First you must learn to play by the rules, then you must forget the rules and play from your heart.

—Unknown

There are two ways to date. You can either date intelligently by being selective about who you choose to date and keeping your standards, or you can practice brainless dating. This is dating anyone who asks and becoming centered on your boyfriend or girlfriend.

Activity: Over the next few weeks, observe some couples that you know. You don't have to set aside specific time to do this, just be aware when you are around them. They can be teenagers or adults. What do you see about them that you admire as a couple? What do you see that you hope you never do when you are in a relationship? Why? What makes them "intelligent daters" or not? Record your thoughts below.

What I Admire and Why

_____

_____

_____

_____

_____

What I Don't Admire and Why

_____

_____

_____

_____

_____

Intelligent Daters? Why or Why Not?

_____

_____

_____

_____

Part of intelligent dating is having a plan. Try the next activity for a way to set up your most important intelligent-dating plan.

Activity: In the space below, write one personal commitment statement for each of the 6 Guidelines to Intelligent Dating. In other words, write a few sentences for how you will personally fulfill these guidelines. Be as specific as possible. This will become your guide and plan that you should review each time you have a date!

Intelligent-Dating Guidelines

My Personal Commitments

Don't date too young. Example: I won't date until I'm 16.

_____

_____

Date people your own age.

_____

_____

DATING+SEX
4

Get to know lots of people.

Date in groups.

Set your own boundaries.

Have a plan.

That last one is really the most important, and filling out this worksheet gets you most of the way there! You should always have a plan for what you are going to do (or not do!) on your date. Always have your ideal plan and at least one backup in case things don't go the way you expect them to.

Activity: Invite three or four friends over (they can be both boys and girls) for a date-planning party. Brainstorm lots of cool ideas for dates, and also think of some plans for how to get through the date—both the "ideal" date and some great backups. Don't forget the treats!

Great Date Ideas

_____

_____

_____

_____

My Ideal Plans

_____

_____

_____

_____

My Backup Plans

_____

_____

_____

_____

Extra Credit! Go to the _6 Decisions_ Web site (www.6decisions.com) and check out the dating ideas you find there. Add some of your own!

Activity: Keeping the idea in mind that you should only date people who respect your standards and make you a better person when you are with them, make a list of people (fill in as many as you can) you know right now who would fit that bill. What's stopping you from asking one of them out? Give it a shot. The worst that can happen is that they'll say no, and that's their loss. If that happens, move on to the next person on your list!

People Who Respect My Standards

1. _____

2. _____

3. _____

4. _____

5. _____

6. _____

7. _____

It's important to know that sometimes relationships can go bad and become very harmful for one or both of the people involved. There are right and wrong ways to get out of an abusive relationship. Here are a few:

- Don't meet the person alone or in a private place.

- Tell others what you are going to do and when.

- Find a person who can support you in your decision.

- Get help in dealing with your feelings after you break up.

Activity: If you are in an abusive relationship, make your plan for breaking up and write it below. If you're not in an abusive relationship, make a plan just in case you find yourself (or a friend) there someday.

When I Will Break Up

_____

_____

_____

_____

Where I Will Do It

_____

_____

_____

_____

What I Will Say

_____

_____

_____

_____

Person I Will Tell

_____

_____

How I Will Get Help

_____

_____

_____

The Four Great Sex Myths ——————

(If they're so great, then why are they myths?)

Okay, this is the part where I am going to recommend you go back to the book and do some reviewing. Pages 196–212 cover the really serious stuff. Please take the time to read this section, especially if you haven't already done it. You'll be glad you did!

Here are a couple of ways to keep this information in mind.

Activity: Write the Four Great Sex _Facts_ in your planner, on your mirror, or on a sticky note in your locker, just somewhere you will see them regularly.

THE FOUR GREAT SEX MYTHS	FACTS
1. Everyone's doing it.	Everyone's not doing it.
2. Your sex drive is so strong you can't control it.	You can control your urges.
3. Safe sex is safe.	There's no such thing as safe sex!
4. It's no big deal.	Sex is a very big deal.

If you want to learn more, go to pages 195–212 in the _6 Decisions_ book.

Love Waits

(And waits and waits and . . .)

You've probably heard that patience is a virtue. Well it is, and it's really one of the most important virtues you can have for a number of reasons! Sometimes it just seems unfair that you are continually told to wait for "true love" before you have sex, when every part of your mind and body is telling you otherwise. But there are some pretty compelling reasons for waiting.

Have you had much experience babysitting? Even if you've done it just a few times, think about what it was like. Did you have fun? Played with the kids, then put them to bed? Watched TV the rest of the night? That kind of thing?

Activity: During the next week or so, carefully observe some parents with small children. Think about what their day is like. If you know them well, you might even ask to take care of a baby or small child (or two). Write down some of the things you observe.

Activity: Ask your parents what it was like when you were a baby. Ask them to be honest. You want the good, the bad, and the ugly. Now draw a picture of all the things a baby requires.

People often ask me, "What's the difference between couplehood and babyhood?" in a word? Moisture. Everything in my life is now more moist. Between your spittle, your diapers, your spit-up and drool, you got your baby food, your wipes, your formula, your leaky bottles, sweaty baby backs, and numerous other untraceable sources—all creating an ever-present moistness in my life, which heretofore was mainly dry.

—Paul Reiser, *Babyhood*

Deciding to have sex now can affect other areas of your life as well. Think about some of the consequences—STDs, horrible rumors, and emotional trauma that you might not expect. In a way, the effects of your choice to wait for sex or not is kind of like a chain of dominoes. But you have the power to stop the domino effect. Try this one.

Activity: Create a big domino chain (careful there!). Label each of the dominoes, except the first one, with the perfect plan for your life—things like graduate from high school, go to college, travel. Now, think of the first domino as "have sex now" and give it a push. Pretty easy for all that planning to come crashing down around you, isn't it?

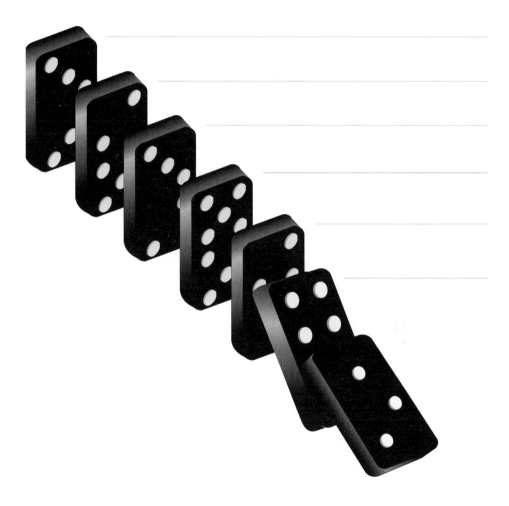

Activity: Go to www.greattowait.com and check out all the resources available to you.

True Love ———————————————

(So near and yet so far)

I know it seems like forever away, but you'll find true love sooner than you think. It's not easy to wait, but taking the high road when it comes to this most important decision will pay off in the end. Hang in there and be smart—about dating, about sex, and about love. You can do it!

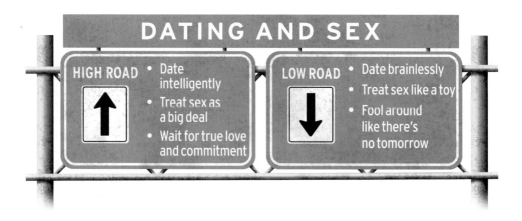

DATING AND SEX

HIGH ROAD ↑	LOW ROAD ↓
• Date intelligently	• Date brainlessly
• Treat sex as a big deal	• Treat sex like a toy
• Wait for true love and commitment	• Fool around like there's no tomorrow

Top 10 Lists

Top 10 Fun Things to Do on a Date

Top 10 People I'd Like to Date

Top 10 Reasons to Wait for Sex

_____

_____

_____

_____

_____

_____

_____

_____

_____

_____

My Top 10 . . .

_____

_____

_____

_____

_____

_____

_____

_____

_____

Favorite Lists

Favorite Romantic Movies

Favorite Love Songs

Favorite Valentine Gifts to Give (and Get)

HOW AM I DOING?

CHECK YOUR CHOICE	TO DO	DOING	DONE
Dating and Sex Checkup	☐	☐	☐
Romantic Movie Scene	☐	☐	☐
6 Universal Dating Questions	☐	☐	☐
Video Dating Game	☐	☐	☐
Dating Experiences	☐	☐	☐
Intelligent Daters	☐	☐	☐
Intelligent-Dating Commitments	☐	☐	☐
Date-Planning Party	☐	☐	☐
People I Want to Date	☐	☐	☐
Get Out of an Abusive Relationship	☐	☐	☐
Four Great Sex *Facts*	☐	☐	☐
What a Baby Requires	☐	☐	☐
Dominoes	☐	☐	☐
Resource Check	☐	☐	☐

DECISION
5

ADDiCTiONS

It's Not Hard to
Quit...I've Done
It a Dozen Times

What's in it
for Me?

1. Ways to help stay on the high road and free of addictions.

2. Healthy alternatives to addictions.

You do anything long enough to escape the habit of living until the escape becomes the habit.

—David Ryan

BRIGHT IDEA!

Ask your parents to read this section of the book! *All* of it! Sometimes teens know more about addictions than parents do. Here's your chance to educate them.

Whoever said that teenagers have it easy is nuts. I'm figuring my *6 Decisions* book and this workbook should be required reading for all adults. That's not to say that adults have it easy either, but sometimes adults don't have a clue about what teens really go through on their path to adulthood.

It is easier to resist at the beginning than at the end.

—Leonardo da Vinci

As you go through this section of the workbook, choose the activities that will arm you the best so that you can resist peer pressure, temptation, and experimentation now, when it's a little easier. If you open the floodgates, even just once, you never know how much harder resisting can be.

i did it to myself. it wasn't society . . . it wasn't a pusher, it wasn't being blind or being black or being poor. it was all my doing.

—Ray Charles, on his heroin addiction

 **ADDICTIONS CHECKUP**

CIRCLE YOUR CHOICE	NO WAY!				HECK YES!
1. I have made up my mind that I will never use drugs.	1	2	3	4	5
2. I am free of any compulsive behaviors such as gambling, shopping, overeating, Web surfing, or endless TV watching.	1	2	3	4	5
3. When it comes to choices about alcohol, tobacco, and drugs, I make my own decisions and don't give in to peer pressure.	1	2	3	4	5
4. I have been alcohol and tobacco free for the last 30 days.	1	2	3	4	5
5. I avoid situations where there's going to be heavy drinking or drugs.	1	2	3	4	5
6. I stay away from Internet porn.	1	2	3	4	5
7. I hang out with friends who share my views about substance abuse.	1	2	3	4	5
8. I encourage my friends to stay away from harmful substances.	1	2	3	4	5
9. I never let my friends drink and drive.	1	2	3	4	5
10. I am free of any eating disorders such as anorexia or bulimia.	1	2	3	4	5
TOTAL					

Add up your score and see how you're doing.

 You're on the high road. Keep it up!

 You're straddling the high and low roads. Move to higher ground!

 You're on the low road. Pay special attention to this chapter.

Three Brutal Realities

(Are you ready?)

When I was a teenager, I remember feeling totally invincible. Nothing was going to hurt me, stop me, or get in my way. I know now that it wasn't true then, just like it isn't even true now! We all have strengths and weaknesses. But saying no to drugs and alcohol is not a sign of weakness. It's a sign of strength. It's a sign that you know who you are and what you want out of life. It's a sign that you know drugs and alcohol can keep you from having those things.

Activity: First, make a list of some hard moments that you have or think you might one day face.

Hard Moments

1. Example: Friday nights after the football game when everyone is hanging out.

_____

2. _____

_____

_____

3. _____

_____

_____

Now make a list of the specific ways you will stay strong in the hard moments. Are there ways you can avoid the hard moments yourself? What are they? Write your answers in the space below.

How I Can Avoid the Hard Moments

1. Example: Plan a get-together with friends at my house.

_____

2. _____

_____

3. _____

_____

Three Great "Thanks, But No Thanks" Responses

1. Example: No way, dude. My parents have spies everywhere.

_____

2. _____

_____

3. _____

_____

No, it's Not Just About You ————————

i am not addicted to nicotine.
Why must i participate in your drug addiction?

—Ken Faver

Whether it's nicotine from secondhand smoke or the emotional impact of living with an addict, addiction touches more people than you think.

Activity: In the wheels below, write the names of the people who would be impacted if you picked up an addiction. If you already have an unhealthy addiction, write the names of those you're impacting now.

If you want to learn more, go to pages 228–235 in the *6 Decisions* book.

It's important to know that nobody sets out to become an addict. Smoking, drinking, and doing drugs may seem harmless if you just try them once, but they are NOT! The addiction train is always right around the corner from a painful and horrible crash, and you never know when it will hit.

Activity: List some things that are important to you. What things would you be willing to trade for an addiction? Because when you pick up an addiction, you are trading the things that are important to you for the addiction. Get it?

IMPORTANT TO ME	WILLING TO TRADE FOR ADDICTION	
1. My little brother or sister's trust	Yes _____	No _____
2. My boyfriend or girlfriend	Yes _____	No _____
3. My car	Yes _____	No _____
4. My future	Yes _____	No _____
5. My reputation	Yes _____	No _____
6. My job	Yes _____	No _____
7. My grades	Yes _____	No _____

8. Other things:

_____

_____

_____

_____

_____

_____

The Truth, the Whole Truth, and Nothing But

(This is serious stuff.)

Ever hear the saying "The truth shall set you free"? Well, there is something to be said for that. If you're not educated about the effects of addictions, how can you possibly make good choices?

Sometimes just living daily life can seem like a brutal reality or truth, but the long-term consequences of trying to mask or cover up the difficulties of life by using drugs and alcohol are by far more difficult to overcome.

Activity: Choose some of the facts below and give your friends and parents a true/false quiz.

1. Beer and wine are safer than liquor.

2. Smokeless tobacco (chew) is safer to use than cigarettes.

3. The marijuana sold today is stronger than when you (your parents) were a teen.

4. Prescription drugs are safer than street drugs.

5. If someone slipped you a club drug, you would know it right away.

6. Steroids stay in your system for about a week.

7. One huff of an inhalant can kill you.

8. Drugs that stay in your system for only a short time are less addictive than others.

9. Crystal meth is like using a diet pill.

How did they do? To find out more information about these facts, go to pages 235–248 in the *6 Decisions* book.

> **Everybody smokes! Models, actresses, everyone!**
> **Don't they realize that it's gross?**
> **i understand it's an addiction,**
> **but it still pains me to see my friends do it.**
>
> —Kirsten Dunst

Answers:
1. False
2. False
3. True
4. False
5. False
6. False
7. True
8. False
9. False

Activity: Create a logo or make an ad for an antitobacco campaign.

Extra credit! Share your logo or ad with your class or submit it to a national antitobacco organization.

Activity: Check out the following Web sites and learn some new things about tobacco addiction. Write what you learned here. Now choose some different sites and discover ways to break the tobacco addiction. If you have a friend who smokes, share what you learned with him or her.

www.notobacco.org

www.thetruth.com

www.tobaccofacts.org

Striking at the Root

(No, we are not talking about hair color here.)

No one ever starts out thinking, "I can't wait to become an addict." When's the last time you heard someone say it was on their list of long-term goals? I would bet never. The reason people become addicted is they have a deeper need that is not being met. It may not be apparent right away, but if you dig deep enough, it's there.

Activity: See if you see yourself in any of the Roots of Addiction below. If you do, write about how you think it applies to you.

The Roots of Addiction

I feel insecure and want to belong.

My friends are doing it and I feel pressured by them.

I am trying to hide pain from the past, like a death in the family, a divorce, or being abused.

I feel confined and want to rebel.

I want to escape from my current problems.

I'm bored or curious.

This is how _____ **applies to me:**

[List Root of Addiction here]

_____

_____

_____

_____

_____

_____

If you found yourself fitting into any of the roots on the previous page, it's time to find some healthy addictions. Those are things that can give you a natural and healthy high.

Activity: Make a poster or collage (be creative!) of all the things you can do for a healthy high. Post it in your room. If you're struggling for ideas, think of things like shooting hoops, reading a book, or going for a hike. If you need to, make a list of your healthy highs to get you started.

Things I Can Do for a Healthy High

Activity: Based upon the "3 Knows" listed below, make a plan for how you will live by these three things.

Know the Facts

My Plan

_____

_____

_____

_____

_____

_____

_____

_____

_____

_____

Know Yourself

My Plan

_____

_____

_____

_____

Know the Situation

My Plan

Drugs and alcohol aren't the only addictive substances out there. You can become addicted to anything if you do it too much. You might think you can beat anything that comes your way, but play around with an addiction, and you'll find out that it will take away your freedom to choose.

Activity: In the space below, figure out how much time you spend on the computer or watching TV during the week.

My Computer/TV Time Log

Monday _____

Tuesday _____

Wednesday _____

Thursday _____

Friday _____

Saturday _____

Sunday _____

Things I Will Do This Week Instead of Spending My Time on the Computer

Example: Play tennis with my cousin.

_____

_____

_____

_____

_____

_____

_____

_____

_____

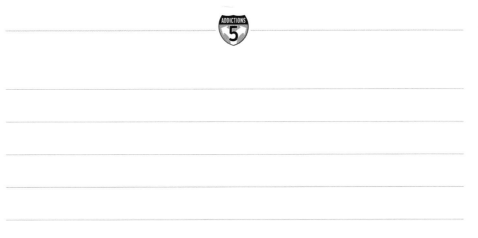

Staying away from addictions is easier when you have a goal or plan in place. It doesn't have to be detailed, but being specific about what you want, what you want to be like, and how you are going to get there really helps.

Activity: Through whatever medium you prefer (writing, art, music), create a picture of how you see yourself 10 years from now if you let your addictions decide what you do with your life. If you choose to draw or write, you can do it below.

10 Years from Now with Addictions

Now do the same thing, visualizing how you see yourself if you stay away from addictions.

10 Years from Now Addiction-Free

Which "Picture" Do You Like Best? Why?

Energy is the essence of life. Every day you decide
how you're going to use it by knowing what you
want and what it takes to reach that goal,
and by maintaining focus.

—Oprah Winfrey

This has been a pretty heavy chapter, I know. But there's nothing funny about addiction. Nothing. If you're already taking the high road (no pun intended) and are addiction-free, give yourself a high five! If you're not, it's time to get back on the right path. Get help and get your life back. You'll be glad you did.

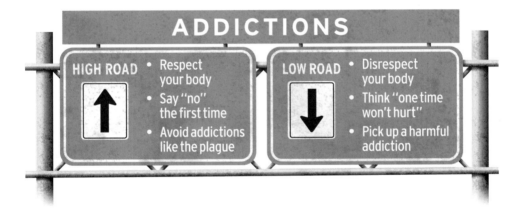

Top 10 Lists

**Top 10 Reasons Why I Choose to Stay
Away from Alcohol, Tobacco, and Drugs**

Top 10 Stupid Excuses for Doing Drugs, Tobacco, and Alcohol

Top 10 Ways to Say No

My Top 10 . . .

Favorite Lists

Favorite Drug-Free and Alcohol-Free Things to Do with My Friends

Favorite One-liners to Say No to Drugs and Alcohol

Favorite Bands or Singers Who Advocate a Drug-Free Life

HOW AM I DOING?

CHECK YOUR CHOICE	TO DO	DOING	DONE
Addictions Checkup	☐	☐	☐
Hard Moments	☐	☐	☐
People Impacted	☐	☐	☐
What's Important to You?	☐	☐	☐
True/False Quiz	☐	☐	☐
Create a Logo or an Ad	☐	☐	☐
Online Research	☐	☐	☐
Roots of Addictions	☐	☐	☐
Things I Can Do for a Healthy High	☐	☐	☐
The 3 Knows	☐	☐	☐
Computer Time	☐	☐	☐
Visualize Your Future	☐	☐	☐

What's in it
for Me?

1. Why it's not healthy to obsess about other people's opinions of me.

2. A practical approach to building self-worth.

3. Ideas for ways to handle the thorns of life that so easily get in my way.

BRIGHT IDEA!

Go to the *6 Decisions* Web site (www.6decisions.com) and see what others have done to boost their self-worth. Add your own ideas.

Self-Worth

To be nobody-but-yourself—in a world which is doing its best, night and day, to make you everybody else—means to fight the hardest battle which any human being can fight; and never stop fighting.

—e e cummings

Just how much are you worth? "Nothin'" is not an answer! You are worth more than you can imagine! This section is really meant to tie all the others together. It's the key to making all of those other choices and decisions. If you feel valued and have a strong sense of self-worth, then you have given yourself the strongest reason for staying on the high road in other ways.

Building your self-worth is an ongoing process because, as the quote says, you will always be subjected to others who are trying to tear you down or make you over. But over time, the stronger your sense of self, the easier it is to maintain. Check out some great ideas for building your confidence in a way that will stick with you for the rest of your life.

Don't think you are, know you are!

—Morpheus, in the film *The Matrix*

 **SELF-WORTH CHECKUP**

CIRCLE YOUR CHOICE	NO WAY!				HECK YES!
1. I generally like myself.	1	2	3	4	5
2. I have confidence in myself.	1	2	3	4	5
3. I'm okay with how I look.	1	2	3	4	5
4. I can handle rude or mean comments.	1	2	3	4	5
5. I have good skills and talents.	1	2	3	4	5
6. I finish what I start.	1	2	3	4	5
7. I am happy for others when they succeed, even those closest to me.	1	2	3	4	5
8. I regularly push myself to try new things and expand my comfort zone.	1	2	3	4	5
9. I see myself as a winner.	1	2	3	4	5
10. I have accomplished some important things in my life.	1	2	3	4	5
TOTAL					

Add up your score and see how you're doing.

 40-50 You're on the high road. Keep it up!

 30-39 You're straddling the high and low roads. Move to higher ground!

 10-29 You're on the low road. Pay special attention to this chapter.

The Social Mirror and the True Mirror—
(Can't live with 'em, can't live without 'em)

The social mirror could be compared to one of those mirrors in the fun house at amusement parks. It's not reality and you don't expect it to be. You expect it to give you a distorted vision of yourself. That's how it is when you let others determine how you should look, act, or feel—the external stuff.

The true mirror is internal. It's the mirror that helps you look inside *yourself* (not through the eyes of others) for how you want to be. It comes from your conscience and self-awareness. The true mirror will project your potential for greatness!

Activity: Okay, I know this activity was in the *6 Decisions* book already, but if you didn't already do it, then choose to do it now! This is the starting point. Answer the questions below.

· THE SOCIAL MIRROR ·

(How would others describe me?)

- _____
- _____
- _____
- _____
- _____

· THE TRUE MIRROR ·

(How would I describe the real me, my best self?)

- _____
- _____
- _____
- _____
- _____

If you want to learn more, go to pages 269–274 in the *6 Decisions* book.

Activity: You know how you *think* others would describe you, but how do you *want* them to describe you? Make your list below.

How I Want Others to Describe Me

The social mirror is unrealistic. It's based entirely on what other people think and do. You know how we tell little kids that things on TV and the movies are "just pretend"? Well, you should remember that too! All movies, TV shows, and books are like that, so don't get upset about never being able to look as good or talk as well as the characters in a movie; if you had someone doing your hair, makeup, wardrobe, and script, you would be just as impressive as any actor!

Activity: Make a list of some of your favorite movies, books, or TV shows. When you watch these shows or read these books, how do you feel afterward?

BOOK/MOVIE/TV SHOW   HOW IT MAKES ME FEEL

_____   _____

_____   _____

_____   _____

_____   _____

Because there are so many TV shows and movies out there, it may seem easy to pick a role model for yourself. Role models can be great things . . . as long as you pick a realistic one. Are you choosing a role model based on the social mirror or the true mirror?

Activity: If you already have a role model, make a list of the reasons why you chose that person. Are they social-mirror things or true-mirror things?

MY ROLE MODEL	REASONS FOR MY CHOICE	SOCIAL MIRROR/ TRUE MIRROR?

Is it time for a change? Who would be a better role model based upon the true mirror?

Activity: Once you have chosen a great role model based on the true mirror, list three qualities that that person has that you want to work on. Make a plan for how you will do this.

TOP THREE QUALITIES	HOW I WILL WORK ON BUILDING THOSE QUALITIES
1. _____	_____
_____	_____
_____	_____
_____	_____
_____	_____
2. _____	_____
_____	_____
_____	_____
_____	_____
3. _____	_____
_____	_____
_____	_____
_____	_____

You may not think you have much power over your life right now, but you do! When you let people's opinions make you self-conscious, you give away your power. It's like handing over the remote control of your life to somebody else. Frequently, what you see on TV, in movies, and on the computer screen can be a big factor in how you see yourself.

Activity: Decrease your computer- and TV-watching time at least one hour every day for a week. List the things you will do to fill your time and then schedule those activities for the upcoming week. Take a look at the activities you listed on page 140 and schedule time next week to complete them on the calendar below.

Monday

Tuesday

Wednesday

Thursday

Friday

Saturday

Sunday

Activity: Every single day, look at yourself in the mirror and say out loud: "I will not compare myself to anyone but myself. I will be comfortable with how I look and focus on my best features." Sounds silly, but it really works!

Activity: Make your own mirror. Buy an inexpensive mirror or find an old one. Using permanent markers, decorate the mirror with positive affirmations and words. If you can't get a real mirror to decorate, use the one below and post it somewhere you will see it every day.

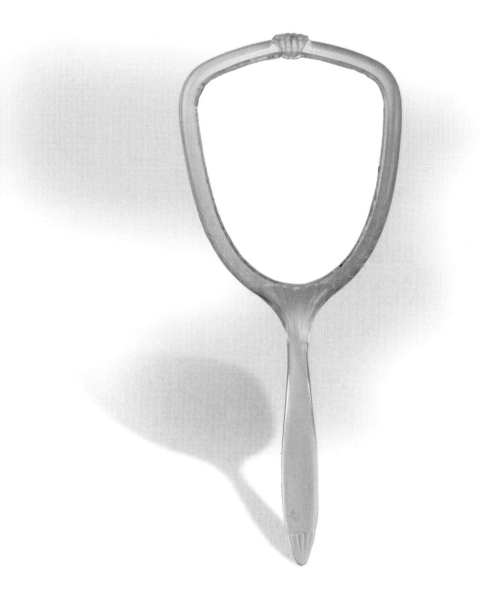

Character and Competence

(The Two Cs)

Character is who you are, the qualities you possess—things like honesty, friendliness, trustworthiness, and cheerfulness. Competence is what you're good at—your talents, skills, and abilities. Together, these qualities make up the core of who you are as a person.

Activity: Choose any four to five people you know and determine where they fall in the Character and Competence Square below. Don't forget yourself! Which people do you admire? Where are you in the square? How can you improve?

THE CHARACTER AND COMPETENCE SQUARE

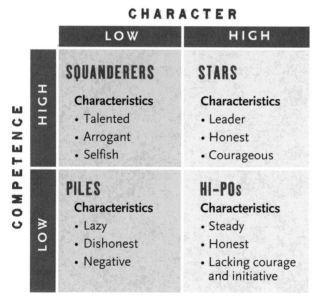

If you want to learn more, go to pages 274–289 in the *6 Decisions* book.

Integrity is the first foundation stone of good character. It's more than being honest. It's about being true to what you know is right and then standing up for that no matter what. It's about being honest with *yourself*. Having a high sense of integrity helps you sleep at night!

Activity: What does integrity mean to you? In what ways do you practice integrity? What can you do to improve?

What Integrity Means to Me

_____

_____

_____

_____

Ways I Practice Integrity

_____

_____

_____

_____

Ways I Can Improve

_____

_____

_____

Activity: Ask your friends, teachers, coaches, parents, and grandparents what integrity means to them.

What Integrity Means to Them

_____

_____

_____

_____

_____

_____

_____

_____

The best way to practice integrity is to practice it every day, one decision at a time. When you say you'll do something, do it!

Activity: Build a wall of integrity around yourself. In the bricks below, list all the words you can think of that define or describe integrity.

INTEGRITY

Activity: List possible situations you could be in where practicing integrity would be important. For each situation, write about how you would feel if you did, or didn't, practice integrity. What are the benefits? What are the drawbacks? Is it worth it? I think if you think about it carefully, you will realize that the answer is it is always better to act with integrity.

Possible Situations

Example: Your friend got the answers to the chemistry test from someone who had the class last year. Your friend offers to share the answers with you.

Never be bullied into silence.
Never allow yourself to be made a victim.
Accept no one's definition of your life; define yourself.

—Harvey Fierstein

Those who bring sunshine into the lives of others, cannot keep it from themselves.

—James M. Barrie, *author of* Peter Pan

Service to others is the second foundation stone of character. We live in a very me-centered world, so this can be a hard one. It takes strength to look outside yourself and see the needs of others. But once you do, you will be amazed at how much better you feel about *yourself*! Give it a try.

Activity: In the foundation stones of character below, list some service opportunities you might be interested in.

The great irony (look it up!) is that building your self-worth often comes when you help someone else build theirs.

Activity: Choose a brother, sister, or friend who seems to be struggling, and share with them some of the ideas you learned in this section.

The third foundation stone of character is faith. Faith is believing in something you can't see, but that you know. There are lots of things you can have faith in: your talents, your skills, your abilities, your family's love for you, and even yourself! Most people think of faith in only the spiritual sense, but it is more than that.

Activity: Make a list of what you have faith in and why. Keep it handy and use it to help you stay strong in the hard moments.

What I Have Faith In

i have one life and one chance to make it count for something. . . . i'm free to choose what that something is, and the something i've chosen is my faith. Now, my faith goes beyond theology and religion and requires considerable work and effort. My faith demands—this is not optional—my faith demands that i do whatever i can, wherever i am, whenever i can, for as long as i can with whatever i have to try to make a difference.

—Jimmy Carter

COMPETENCE

Just as character has foundation stones, so too does competence. It seems pretty easy for others to tell you to love yourself and all of that, and it is. And it's also pretty easy to respond mentally with a "yeah, whatever." Having a strong sense of self-worth isn't just about character. Competence is a big part of it. One of the first ways to start building your feelings of self-worth is to focus on developing a talent or skill of some kind, something that you enjoy and will have fun spending a lot of time on. That's the first foundation stone.

Move out of your comfort zone. You can only grow if you are willing to feel awkward and uncomfortable when you try something new.

—Brian Tracy

Activity: In your journal or planner, on your computer, or right here, make a dream list of all the things you want to learn how to do in the next 10 years. Dream big! Don't let time or money stand in the way of writing down what you really want to be and do.

Big Things I Want to Learn to Do

Activity: Now that you have set up some big dreams, make a list of some little things you'd like to learn—things like how to change a tire, how to make your mom's awesome lasagna, or how to clean the bathroom properly!

Little Things I Want to Learn to Do

You have to expect things of yourself before you can do them.

—Michael Jordan

The second foundation stone of competence is accomplishments. Another way to give yourself power is to accomplish something you set your mind to. It doesn't have to be a huge thing. Start small and see what happens.

Activity: Make a *long* list of all your accomplishments, big or small. What are you good at right now? What are you learning right now? What were you good at when you were a little kid? Dig deep and come up with that great big list. I want to see 20 things on this list!

My Accomplishments

For example: I grow really big pumpkins.

I completed the Level 2 guitar book.

I made all-state in track.

1.

2.

3.

4.

5.

6.

7.

8.

9.

10.

SELF-WORTH
6

11. _____

_____

_____

12. _____

_____

_____

13. _____

_____

_____

14. _____

_____

_____

15. _____

_____

_____

16. _____

_____

_____

17. _____

_____

_____

18. _____

_____

_____

19. _____

_____

_____

20. _____

_____

_____

See? You really are good at a lot of things already.

Activity: Now that you've thought about what you have already accomplished, decide on three things you want to accomplish in the next year. Choose things you haven't done before and stick with them. Write them down, make your plan, and set a deadline. Keep your ideas in your planner, in your journal, on your computer, or in this book.

THREE THINGS I WANT TO ACCOMPLISH   **DEADLINE**

1. _____   _____

2. _____   _____

3. _____   _____

Physical health is the third foundation stone of competence. Why? Because in order to be competent and strong in other areas, you have to have the physical stamina to make it all happen. That goes for eating right, sleeping enough, and taking good care of your body. When you feel physically sharp, you are mentally sharp too.

Activity: Check out "today's specials" below. Which ones are you good at? Which ones could you do better? Circle where you think you fall.

Today's specials

1. Eat breakfast

1 2 3 4 5 6 7 8 9 10

2. Don't try fad diets. They're unsustainable. You'll temporarily lose weight, but gain it all back and more in the long run.

1 2 3 4 5 6 7 8 9 10

3. Eat at least five servings of fruits and vegetables daily. Eat a variety. All kinds are good. ✱

1 2 3 4 5 6 7 8 9 10

4. Eat whole grains, like oatmeal, brown rice, and whole wheat, in place of processed grains, like enriched flour, store bought muffins, and white rice.

1 2 3 4 5 6 7 8 9 10

5. Limit your intake of sugar, processed foods, and fried foods, like pop, sugar cereals, and French fries.

1 2 3 4 5 6 7 8 9 10

6. Get at least two servings of protein each day from meat, chicken, fish, eggs, beans, or soy products.

1 2 3 4 5 6 7 8 9 10

7. Get at least two servings of dairy each day from string or cottage cheese, yogurt, frozen yogurt, or milk.

1 2 3 4 5 6 7 8 9 10

8. Eat some healthy fats each day (fish, nuts, olive oil, sunflower oil, canola oil).

1 2 3 4 5 6 7 8 9 10

9. Spread out your calories. You're better off eating smaller meals throughout the day than eating one big meal at one sitting.

1 2 3 4 5 6 7 8 9 10

10. Drink LOTS of water. ✱

1 2 3 4 5 6 7 8 9 10

Which Three Things Will You Commit to Doing Better Starting Today?

1. _____

_____

_____

2. _____

_____

3. _____

_____

_____

Activity: Using "today's specials" as a guide, think about some improvements you can make in your eating habits. Where do you struggle? How can you improve? Was it easy? Why? What can you do to make it easier?

My Struggles

Example: I love soda, but I know that I drink too much of it.

_____

_____

_____

_____

_____

_____

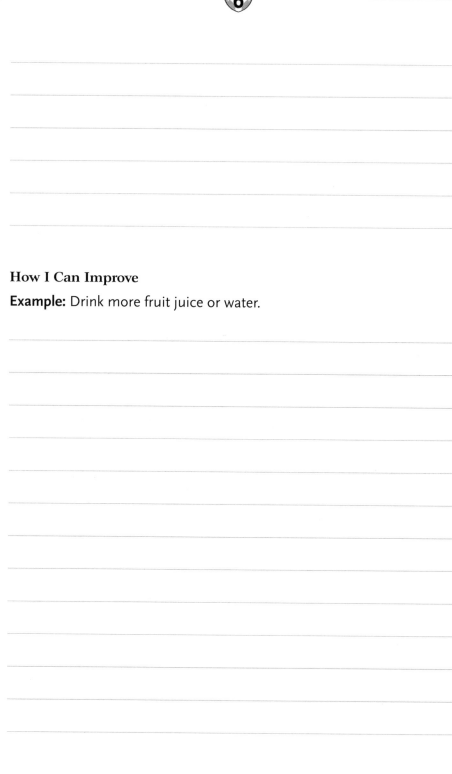

How I Can Improve

Example: Drink more fruit juice or water.

Activity: Get up off the couch and call a friend right now! Ask them to go for a walk or shoot some hoops with you or do some other physical activity. Just get up and get going!

As I said earlier, this section kind of ties all the others together. Smart decision making is the keystone of self-worth. Building a healthy sense of self-worth is the result of being smart about the previous five decisions.

Here's a great reminder for you. You don't have to do anything, just read it!

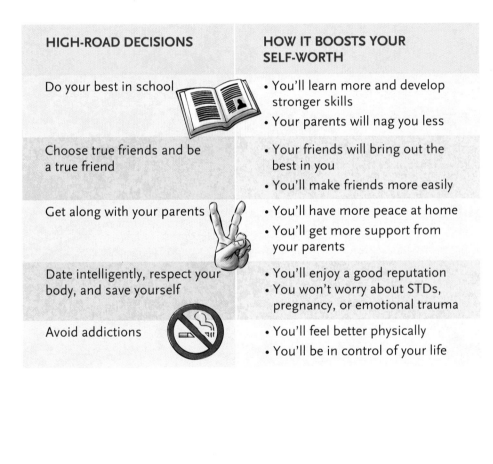

HIGH-ROAD DECISIONS	HOW IT BOOSTS YOUR SELF-WORTH
Do your best in school	• You'll learn more and develop stronger skills • Your parents will nag you less
Choose true friends and be a true friend	• Your friends will bring out the best in you • You'll make friends more easily
Get along with your parents	• You'll have more peace at home • You'll get more support from your parents
Date intelligently, respect your body, and save yourself	• You'll enjoy a good reputation • You won't worry about STDs, pregnancy, or emotional trauma
Avoid addictions	• You'll feel better physically • You'll be in control of your life

**Your work is to discover your world and
then with all your heart give yourself to it.**

—Buddha

Conquering Your El Guapo ————

(El What-o?)

El Guapo. A big dangerous "thing" that needs to be conquered; a hurdle, a struggle. Get it? There are all kinds of El Guapos, and yours are probably not the same as the kid who sits next to you in math class.

Activity: What are your personal El Guapos? By focusing on what you can control, what can you do to overcome them? Record your thoughts and plan below.

MY EL GUAPOS

Example: My parents' divorce.

HOW I MIGHT OVERCOME THEM

Share my feelings with my parents.

If you want to learn more, go to pages 289–300 in the *6 Decisions* book.

You may not realize it when it happens, but a kick in the teeth may be the best thing in the world for you.

—Walt Disney

Building a healthy sense of self-worth doesn't mean you won't ever get hurt or feel insecure. Life is a journey and you have a long way to go. You might get hurt along the way, and that's okay. Learn to believe in yourself, develop a strong sense of self-worth and you will be able to weather the storms and come out on top!

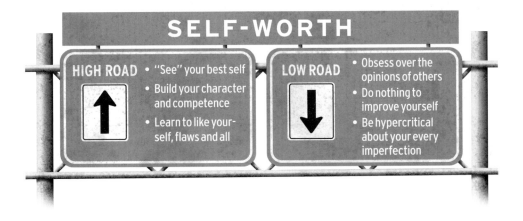

Top 10 Lists

Top 10 Great Things About Me

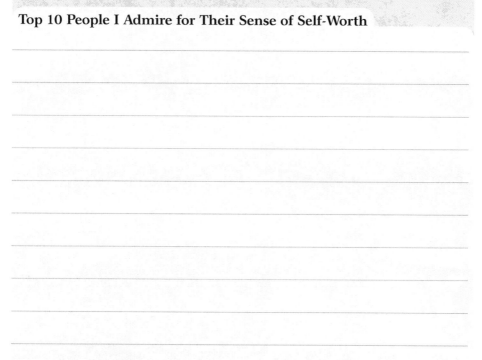

Top 10 People I Admire for Their Sense of Self-Worth

Top 10 Things I Will Do to Increase My Self-Worth

My Top 10 . . .

Favorite Lists

Favorite Movies That Make Me Feel Good About Myself

Favorite Music That Makes Me Feel Good About Myself

Favorite Quotes That Build My Sense of Self-Worth

HOW AM I DOING?

CHECK YOUR CHOICE	TO DO	DOING	DONE
Self-Worth Checkup	☐	☐	☐
Social Mirror, True Mirror	☐	☐	☐
How I Want Others to Describe Me	☐	☐	☐
Favorites List	☐	☐	☐
Role Models	☐	☐	☐
Quality Building	☐	☐	☐
Schedule Quality Time	☐	☐	☐
Make Your Own Mirror	☐	☐	☐
Character and Competence Square	☐	☐	☐
What Integrity Means to Me and Others	☐	☐	☐
Build a Wall of Integrity	☐	☐	☐
Situation Review	☐	☐	☐
Build a Wall of Service	☐	☐	☐
Help Another	☐	☐	☐
Build a Wall of Faith	☐	☐	☐
Things I Want to Learn to Do	☐	☐	☐
My Accomplishments	☐	☐	☐
Three Things I Want to Accomplish	☐	☐	☐
Today's Specials	☐	☐	☐
Improvements to Today's Specials	☐	☐	☐
Get Up and Get Going	☐	☐	☐
My Personal El Guapos	☐	☐	☐

STiCK CODE
TO THE
It's Worth Fighting For!

Although Jack Sparrow in the *Pirates of the Caribbean* movie was talking about a different "code" when he told his mates to "stick to the code," it's still a great line!

You get to choose the code you want to live by, and I hope you're going to choose the high-road code. When you come to those forks in the road, be strong and choose the things you know are right—the things that will lead you to a happy, successful future. It will be tough at times, life just is that way. But you can do it because you *do* have a choice!

Choice makes you who you are. Remember the six biggest choices that you will be faced with, and think about how those six decisions can make or break you. Choose your road wisely, hang on for the ride, and move forward in your life with energy and excitement!

Hopefully, you have completed a lot of the activities in this workbook. If you have, you'll be even more prepared to answer these questions when they come up:

1. What am I going to do about my education?
2. What type of friends will I choose and what kind of friend will I be?
3. What kind of relationships will I build with my parents?
4. Who will I date and what will I choose do to about sex?
5. What will I do about smoking, drugs, pornography, and other addictive things?
6. What am I going to do about building my self-worth?

If you feel like you've already strayed off the high road, don't worry. It's never too late to start making good choices and to make good changes. You can learn from your mistakes and help others learn too. If you're on the high road, you have the opportunity to be an example to others right now. Be a good influence! You'll be glad you did.

Congratulations for all the effort you've made so far! Keep it up and best of luck to you!

Mr. CEO,
I have some thoughts
on how to create a
more sustainable
work environment
for your company.
I can meet with you
anytime after gym class.
Regards,
Devan

Learning today.
Leading tomorrow.

Make sure your kids have the tools to thrive
in a constantly changing world.

The
Leader in Me™

great happens here

www.theleaderinme.org

FranklinCovey   Education Solutions